PIT LULLABIES

Jessica Traynor was born in Dublin in 1984 and is a poet, essayist and librettist. Her debut collection, *Liffey Swim* (Dedalus Press, 2014), was shortlisted for the Strong/Shine Award and in 2016 was named one of the best poetry debuts of the past five years on Bustle.com. Her second collection, *The Quick*, was a 2019 *Irish Times* poetry choice. *A Place of Pointed Stones*, a pamphlet commissioned by Offaly County Council,was published by The Salvage Press in 2021. Her third collection, *Pit Lullabies*, was published by Bloodaxe in 2022.

She has received commissions for poems from BBC Radio 4, The Arts Council of Ireland, The Model Gallery Sligo, The Salvage Press, VISUAL Carlow, Dún Laoghaire–Rathdown County Council and *The Poetry Programme* (RTÉ), and awards including the Hennessy New Writer of the Year, the Ireland Chair of Poetry Bursary, and the Listowel Poetry Prize. In 2016, she was named one of the 'Rising Generation' of poets by Poetry Ireland.

She reviews poetry for RTÉ's *Arena*, and for *Poetry Ireland Review*, and has held residencies including the Yeats Society, Sligo, and Carlow College. She is an inaugural Creative Fellow of UCD, where she completed her MA in Creative Writing in 2008, and is Dún Laoghaire–Rathdown Writer in Residence for 2021-22.

Her website is www.jessicatraynor.com

JESSICA TRAYNOR

Pit Lullabies

BLOODAXE BOOKS

Copyright © Jessica Traynor 2022

ISBN: 978 1 78037 606 6

First published 2022 by
Bloodaxe Books Ltd,
Eastburn,
South Park,
Hexham,
Northumberland NE46 1BS

www.bloodaxebooks.com
For further information about Bloodaxe titles
please visit our website and join our mailing list
or write to the above address for a catalogue.

Supported using public funding by
**ARTS COUNCIL
ENGLAND**

Cover design: Neil Astley & Pamela Robertson-Pearce.

Printed in Great Britain by Bell & Bain Limited, Glasgow, Scotland, on
acid-free paper sourced from mills with FSC chain of custody certification.

Here's a song
from deep in the hole...

CHRIS GOSS

CONTENTS

PIT LULLABY

A whisper in your ear as you sleep —
when I was carrying you,
and you were an electrical storm,
a clump of eels behind the gut,
I cursed a man.

I called all of my demons down
from their rookeries to carry your shock
of legs and stingers to latch onto him.
He thrashed till the whole writhing mess
sank back into a bog pool,
silted, silent.

We witches aren't world-beaters my darling,
we're a needle through the thimble,
the gape of a paper-cut,
mild misfortune
whose sorrow
is always
absorbed.

Megalodon

In gaping mandibles
    the hypnotic interplay
of hinge/ hole
      the sharpened frill
around the brink

what will be left of us
      is these spaces
thresholds   holloways
    paths worn in chalk
releasing Jurassic plankton
      to a summer's day

the dish of my pelvis
      I've served to lovers
    opened for my child –
these pre-historic jaws
    this entry/exit
      & all that thrashes
in its teeth.

Anatomy Scan

Let's begin with a shroud, darkened by time,
pushed aside to show your bones' filigree.
The ultrasound probes and digs as you slither
in and out of focus, sockets gaping
like a Halloween ghost through a sheet.
The hole of your stomach. The chomp
of your heartbeat hungering below my gut.
Perfect cerebellum. A very nice spine.
There – the kidneys. Little dark pockets of need.
Colour flares across the screen, arterial flow
through widening chambers, its rush exhausting.
The eyeball's orbit. Closed but watchful.
Your twig arms flinch and flick. Your tiny jaws grin.
Little lizard. You know something I've forgotten.

In the Birthing Room

The choir sings   pitchy and off-key
but still my hands grasp   flutter
          try to shape   these unruly phrases
till the drag of morphine   collapses them
          I can't read the singers' faces
          behind their masks
          and the lighting is bad –
pale green gowns   glinting implements
          very post-modern   post-dramatic
                    but they won't stand still   one soloist
bends over me   very quiet   very serious
          and the music must be good because
                    I feel something tug in me –
          a root that shouldn't be disturbed
don't cry   you're the conductor
                    then for some reason
I'm given a prize
          but it's a baby   her eyes black
          we look at each other
there must be some mistake
          before she's taken away
                    it's quiet
          when the clean up team arrives
          there is so much blood
                    I'm sorry, but do you know if I've been cut?
                    Of course you have, they say

Metaphysical Breast Milk Poem

Since you were pulled from me   I'm pulped
          bones all spun inside this old skin-coat
now I wake to your cries   in a milk fever
                    curled inside a wreath of womb-blood
caffeine-sweat   wracked with shivers
          I clamp you to my breast
          where your nip   is the pinch
of the universe   squeezing into existence
          the camel passing   through the needle's eye
the hinge of our bodies
          yours all potential
                              mine all emptied bottles
it seems right that this should hurt

Ophelia in Ballybough

October afternoons I walk, baby in sling,
sun glinting on the copper of my filament.
I pace a slow circuit: Clonliffe Road,
Richmond Road, Fairview Park...

In sunlight I'm spectral,
Ophelia haunting an orbit.
Wild things reveal themselves.
A stalking heron. Treecreepers.
On the playing fields beside the Tolka,
a flock of Canada Geese.

*

In my living room I flex my haunches –
kinked a little closer to the feral,
the bones of my house shudder about me.
The night steals my pelt. Everything gets in.

*

The baby learns the corners of her body
by torturous increments.
I hold her like some marvellous fish,
terrified she might slip from my grasp,
drown in this new element.

*

On a golden day in October,
she sleeps against my chest;
I sing *Lavender's Blue* to her
on the empty pitch on Richmond Road.

Crossing the Luke Kelly bridge,
I narrate snowy egrets
picking their way through tidal mud.
Two kingfishers burst from the bridge,
cast
      against the river's flow.

I record these symbols,
this slippage in the order of things,
the brown trout swimming upstream.

I think of Ophelia in her madness,
speaking in tongues of the hedgerow:
fennel, columbine, pansy, rue...

*

The weather turns.
The public health nurse calls.
Storm Ophelia bruises the sky.

*

The baby dozes in her bouncy chair.
We expect the train on the railway line
above our house to come
careening off its track.
But though the storm churns gulls
in its cauldron,
our high-walled yard is silent.

*

I wheel the pram through Fairview Park,
skirt the broken limbs of trees.
A fallen beech blocks my path,

the mysteries of its root-bole coughed up,
standing shocked against low clouds –
another Ophelia toppled. *For some,*
the very worst thing has happened.

*

Our bones reknit in their own crooked way.
I wheel the baby home. The days darken
into winter, lose their electric gleam,
the moon skips back into her orbit.

Midwinter

No sun this morning, but the promise of a tilt
and so men on the radio talk about things we can't see.
Plaques and residues are tangling themselves
around your brain like triskels on Newgrange granite,
but the baby has found the cockles of her fists
and is unspiralling their curls
into darting cuttlefish.

We only talk about this: the things we can see,
the things that are certain –
the baby's wriggle when we sing to her, her liquid grin,
and not the shadows in the corner of the room,
the bright blooms on the negative of your CT scan,
the dark mornings to come.

PIT LULLABY II

a woman haunts your cradle
      I wake in the bone light
      of morning
the air
      troubled   with her passing

you heave sobs
    who honey
        who frightened you

      witch you shout
                       learning sounds
            as they burst from you –

                 you cup the word   like a bird
corpse
                        found stiffened
                in a hedgerow   while I
plead

        witch don't drag us
        with you
    don't give
my daughter
    your name
    for her first word.

A Plea for the Sanctification of the Ditches of Ireland

Ashamed of what I loved
I flung her from me and called her a ditch

PATRICK KAVANAGH, 'Innocence'

In these difficult cases
         where the death-site is unknown –
where guesswork festoons each hedgerow
         bog hole
                  car boot
                           in caution tape
         for a mother sucked through the estuary's throat
and into the sea –

in these dark times when our men
         are driven   by swallowed sorrows
to make a butcher's block   of the hearth
the best course of action
                           is to sanctify the sites
         where these unfortunate women   found their rest.

If we worship them here
         maybe their fractured ribs will knit
like a Moses basket to shelter the heart;
         contusions to the chest
                           legs
                                    forearms

will fade like darkness licked back
         into an inky horizon;   broken necks
will kink into place with a click
                           as neat as a car boot's closing

21

and mirrored   in the meadow's satin dew
        will be a host of little Virgins
                mothers of the field
                                ditch
                                        cistern.

Each little break-neck   each strangled waif
        will be May Queen
        a fly-tipped boreen her altar
                and her voice will pour like honey
over the fields   sweet as blackbird song
        rippling the wooded glen –

Oh raise your hands in supplication
        chant her name   across the evening in a round:

        Mother ditch prepare a bed for us
                among the nettle leaves
        O mother dip your net for us
                amongst the choppy waves
        O mother ditch we pine for you
                until the moon is full
        and then we see your face appear
                in every bog pool...

Child you cut me open

my body a midden
          of rosehips
withered sloes
              keys and coins
     that clank about.

     These fragments
              can't survive.
Even November's
     lemon-water sunlight
blanches them   bone white
     and I'm not sure
I can live
     without these secrets
              shut inside –

but then you turn your gaze
          to the shadowlands
behind my head
          smile   at the ghosts
that hover
          by my shoulders
till all
     their chains
              unknot.

What It Takes

for those who have suffered birth injuries

There is a curse on us it's true
but not for the theft of a rib
        or an apple bite
or because we want to grasp
        the snake's rough muscle

it's what it takes   to split in two
        release the new into the world
to teach four seasons   when all
we will remember
is snow fall   soft
        the time when everyone
has gone and we are left

        imagining heartbeats
    in rooms that thrum with absence
the relay race   we never asked to run
        our thoughtless cells
    carrying messages
of love –

illegible letters   in the kink of a brow,
the slope of a cheekbone   that say:

I once loved this man and let him slide inside my life until we both
forgot ourselves and left to the world the image of our atoms locked
together in a creation so complete it houses worlds; halls and cupboards,
saucers, eggcups, stained glass windows, graveyards and gardens where
blind roots slip between bricks

but what this takes   is everything
        our only measurable success   not dying
until we do

Patchwork Quilt

The baby gathers the blanket
  its tiny fields
as if she could pick the oceans up
    fold them in a box.

Whole towns
  are swept into her arms,
cities with their skyscrapers
  clenched in clammy fingers.

A herd of palominos
  upended sky becomes sand
    sand air
sea creatures fall skyward

  a whale suspended
by centrifugal force before beginning
    its graceful plummet.

The baby opens her mouth
    chews a fistful of Europe.
Kings and queens
  businessmen witches

commuters trolls tired librarians
  roll around clutching their phones
and compostable cups
  before the merciless gums descend

and the horizon
    turns
      red

If You Can Tame a Wildcat, You Can Raise a Baby

Lesson One
You have no shared contexts –
forget sentimentality.
The child recognises you
as a fox on a winter's night
hears the owl shriek above it.

Lesson Two
Now you have accepted
you have no shared context,
we should admit one –
the seeking of pattern.
Repeat, repeat, repeat
until threat becomes comfort.

Lesson Three
Like any animal, this child
has the capacity for love.
Like any adult, you know
you deserve only contempt.

Lesson Four
The smile is learned,
all mirrors are Antarctic wastes.
But your breath is warm –
write your message on the glass.

Lesson Five
You are both feral,
scavengers haunting
a night of cutthroat stars.
Touch your nose
to the frozen earth,
breathe, breathe each other's scent.

PIT LULLABY III

In the scrub behind the tennis court
you arrange sticks into rough squares.
What are these windows? You look to
the sky, call down magpies, but I look
to the ground, see the gleam of lights
somewhere below, existing, as we do,
in spite of ourselves. You're hoping
to catch the sky in a mirror; its bright
pennants of cloud. I'm hoping not
to fall into the dark.

On Poisons

I *Ditches*

So many songs I could sing you,
spread fields of lavender
for you to crush in your fists.
But there are things more potent
than the peaches and plums
in your story books,
there are shadows in the ditch
that know your name.
Sit with me –
I'll teach you theirs.

II *Giant Hogweed*

Do you find my height a threat?
It's a gift I treasure. Look what I offer –
my white starburst, my firework display

in the gloom of these close August days.
Don't ignore me. Come closer,
use your fingers, feel the heft of my stem

so we can begin our exchange.
What I will give you: a last glimpse
of my flower unfurling

to take with you into darkness,
and a cellular change, a choker of blisters,
that marks you as mine.

III *Yew*

Look for me among tumbled stones –
trace your fingers over skulls, crossed bones,
read the names written there.
The sky spins overhead
while lichens bloom and rhizomes
weave webs between my roots.
My children hang from my branches
in red jackets. Once,
before we withered into silence,
my husband sent a blackbird
to fill his crop with those berries.
The bird's bones hide now
among leaf mould and loam,
thin as my own fallen needles,
stitching year on year.

IV *Hellebore*

Comes to the poison doctor, head down,
a patient who won't look him in the eye –

and while he tries to catch her glance,
he'll miss the aphids gorging on her sap.

As she smiles, her shadow gathers
around his ankles, a pleated skirt

to make him trip on a frost-crisped morning,
send him sprawling to a shattered hip.

And as she pulls him to his feet,
he doesn't feel the sickness gather

at his skull's base, crouch in his spinal column –
Nitrogen dioxide. Mercury. Lead.

Shy beauties bowing in the flower bed.

V *Foxglove*

speckled lecher open
to every passing maggot,
your leopard-print tie dye,
your innocence litmus test
acid-burnt, fooling no one.
There's the pink,
but the black burns through,
with a heave, a gasp –
the writhing pillar
swaying in the breeze,
gale-knocked but springing back,
coiling and uncoiling
till the heart just stops.

VI *Cuckoo Pint*

Find a wood and set your child loose
to forage flowers and berries.
Warn them to steer clear of nettles,
of men who travel alone, or in packs.
Tell them about tetanus, ticks and broken glass,
about hypodermic needles and fly agaric mushrooms,
blackberries glazed with glyphosate,
carrion laced with rat poison.
When you have taught them all the ways
the world will break their fingers,
close the car door, check your weather App.
When they come back you'll know them by what they bring;
if the child carries fistfuls of cuckoo pint,
red berries throbbing through the dusk,
reflecting light onto their hopeful face,
this signifies the child is a bastard,
and not of your flesh.
The clever child will carry nothing but their breath,
because the answer to the riddle
of what is safe is *nothing   no one   nowhere.*

VII *Rue*

Pin me to your breast as an aide-memoir,
to sharpen sight. Keep your wits
about you and if my petals wilt
pull another stem from the bank.
Don't tell your father about the man
who pushed you down into the ditch,
about the way the water billowed your hair.
Follow the well-worn path;
take me to the water,
throw my petals in the stream
singing your crack-voiced ditty:
fennel, columbine, pansy, rue...
stuff your nose with flowers to dull scent
until you see your own body,
white and lithe, slip away from you
like a pale fish, bellied up by the current.
Learn to turn regret into pity
for the limbs you never owned.

VIII *Wolf's Bane*

Oh granny, how tight your bonnet,
how bright the miraculous medal
against liver-spotted skin.

How fearful the hump of your back,
your wren bones that once held
the three girls thrashing to escape you.

How you wait in your bed,
pink tongue lolling, for the men
who would hack through your door

to meet your teeth, dulled but still sharp.
You never knew who deserved your bite;
the woodsman who would club you

till blood tinged clumps of fur,
or the girls in their red hoods
who didn't want your consolation.

IX *Apple Seed*

Bite the core
to find my black eyes.

If you swallow me
I'll root in your gut,

sprout a trunk
to burst from your mouth;

with your last breath –
a shower of petals on the breeze.

PIT LULLABY IV

When you wake in the dark
to find me gone
　　　I'll be standing at the night gate
on Glengall Street
　　　　　the gate you don't notice in daytime
until a pied cat slinks through　　　　　*or the hinges*
　　　　　　whine their small song of neglect.

This is the gate that lets the night through
　　　　　　keeps it out
and I am standing here　　*alone*　　　*in my green army coat*
　　　hair shorn a woman thinned
　　　by so many miles of walking

ready for the ghasts and boggarts that might come through
　　　ready for the moths big as donkeys
　　　　　　that crash towards the moon.

When you are old enough to join me there
I will ask you
　　　　Do you want the night gate
　　　　open
　　　　or shut?

In the Wrong Place

A weed is a flower growing in the wrong place
GEORGE WASHINGTON CARVER

Sprouting up like knotweed
                    impossible to eradicate
            a fragment of hair or bone can germinate
falling in drifts in a stiff breeze
                    rustling like a paper ocean

you'll find them hanging in the kelp forest
            clogging up the plastic ocean
tangling with eels in the Sargasso
            keratin forests of hair ballooning
                    about their bloated faces

        or riddling the earth with their leavings
tunnelling beneath us in darkness
                    scattering ribs and teeth and golden torcs
the leftovers that make up a life

        meaning that crumbles
while the shape remains
            a rusted key   a paper weight
a sweatshirt muddied in the shallows

        and then the particles of skin
and faecal matter we eat and breathe
                    the blood that evaporates
and the tyres that burn

the asbestos that gifts its soft fibres
            our organs marbled with benzene and fat
it can't be good for us
            yet there we hang
                    another crop of us
        ripening

38

Forecast

Meteorologists slit
the throats of geese,
dab their fingers in blood,
smear computer screens
with messages
that outlast the changing news.
A coil of entrails in a bucket
is a closed eye,
betraying nothing.

In a darkened office
at the pyramid's tip
a man consults the annals
and rolls a seven sided dice –

Perhaps this year
will be like 1224, when
there arose a great blast of wind
which fell down the house
of Magnus McMurtagh,
whereof one part fell on the said Magnus
and did put the top of his head
through his brains to his very neck
and caused his neck to sink
into his breast, and strucken dead,

perhaps it will be a year of collapses
and expulsions, when the gall knot
of men on the streets will swell
into a wasp's nest –
their bodies clenching
as summer ripens.

Or the year might be like 1173,
when in Derry,
the dark night was illuminated
from midnight to daybreak,
and the people thought
the neighbouring parts of the world,
which were visible, were in a blaze of light;
the likeness of a large globe of fire arose
over the town and moved
in a south-easterly direction,
and the people rose from their beds
imagining it was daylight.

The meteorologists
scatter knuckle bones.
One licks a finger,
sticks it in the wind.
One idly twirls a wind sock.
Their computers tell them nothing
but crackled messages have been coming
from the lighthouse keepers; the wave,
they say, *the wave is coming*
blotting the horizon, rolling whales
and sea beasts with it towards the land –

and what can the weathermen do,
when this has been foretold
for so long? The barometer
can't control the creeping mercury.

The weathermen chart the changing fronts
until another message
rattles a phone on the table:
The wave is coming – the same refrain,
moving north-westerly
from Hook Head
to Bloody Foreland.

On Plastics

The guy at the till says
can't put that back love,
            it's been touched –
and dumb   I drop the fork
            in the bin   think

oh love   we've all
            been touched   soiled
                  some of us have pushed

whole humans out
            crunching through
                  pelvises
in a gush   of blood   shit

            & some have been hit
stabbed   slit   with pint glasses
surgeon's scalpels

bones cracked   with the butt
            of a blade   by butchers
preparing   a feed of marrow
            for hungry guests

we have touched ourselves
                  our screens
each other on screens

            till bacteria trails
we've traced
                  grow verdant
and when you claw

41

       voluptuous loam
allow worms   leeches
      beetles
          slither your arms

you'll find beneath it all
     that fucking pristine
        plastic fork
outlasting all our snot & puke & tears

Supermoon Trifecta

Super blood wolf moon

In days gone by, all you'd know is the sudden wet sweat smell slick your nostrils. Nerve sing then black. Sometimes the ivory closeness of tooth, blood's warm consolation.

Now, all dressed in red hoods, ridiculous among the sheep sheds like groups of teens, hormones howl bad unsexy sex. Lit up. Illuminated. Caught. *Bad dog* we say, turn back home.

But there are more and more of them each night.

Super snow moon

Whisper silver onto the sea. The earth's fingerprint thrown up into the sky, proving nothing. Sounds so deep you can't hear them.

Somewhere in the vast north, a figure walks through snow. I witness this. It is true, for now, but the song of it, ending, haunts the ice. A kind of release, tectonic fugue, as wolf skulls that have slept for millennia melt and plash.

On Everest, chattering corpses thaw.

Super worm moon

The astronomy lobby are big out here. Got you staring up so they can swipe your bag. Talk talk talk about options for when the ball dries up. We can't see you up there but we hear the sing of you, vibrating through the turf. Skies will fill your head with nonsense. Pointless pricks of light in fecund black. We see nothing but shit. Shit as is and shit as was. Synthetic fibres hard to digest, but we break it all down, only come up once a year. We know the lure of that big whitehead, deceptive tunnelling bastard, pulling us towards a kind of birth. We don't like things that eat their own tail. We move forwards/backwards. Spare us your onwards/upwards. Spare us your equinoctial phases and yellow, jagged beaks. We hear the sing of you in your polyester clothes, stumping around on your hooves. Shit as is and shit as will be.

Walrus

As we strip wallpaper layers
from the box room,
a pattern emerges: the Walrus,
the Carpenter, a chorus of oysters –
pale Alice looks on.

'The time has come,' the Walrus said,
'To talk of many things…

So sleep child in your new room,
second beloved of these walls.
Sleep as the sun rises and ice melts
and for want of the freeze a walrus
pushes further up a cliff-face.

…Of shoes – and ships – and sealing-wax –
Of cabbages – and kings –

Oh egg-man, wallowing uphill,
before tumbling,
pole-synched towards sea,
to join your rock-broken herd
at the cliff-base.

…And why the sea is boiling hot –
And whether pigs have wings.'

Sleep child as I browse washing machines,
and the ball of tears at my throat dribbles
with detergents down the drain.
More beauty broken
in an eyelash-flickered blink
than I can ever tell you.

Men Are Talking

Men are talking to each other
and outside the overheated room
swans stumble, feet bound
to the frozen lake.

Men are talking to each other
and decapitated stags bellow
over the gilt chairs,
wailing walls of brocade.

Men of state
          men of state
                    are talking.

While the newscaster drones
in Greek or Turkish or Russian
the men descant
above her monotone.

They thrust speech into each other,
bodies feats of engineering;
legs spread like girders,
each handshake a buttress.

Outside the hotel/palace/dacha
ice clasps everything in place,
men are talking
          men are talking
                    by the lake.

PIT LULLABY V

Here are some things I need you to know:
this darkness is an absence of light,
and not inklings of soot that fall from space
redacting the sky's pale grey.

It's not a cloud of ink announcing
the movement, deep below,
of a squid who reaches
to grasp the moon's far bead,
or a knuckle of gall
built around us by wasps

It's not a fog released by miners
who tunnelled here for potash
or the surface of a lake
beneath the sea
where even fish drown

It is the pinprick in your pupil
that lets the world in,
the mark I make on paper to name you
the space between you, and those you love.

An Island Sings

I *Song of the Dusk*

What is the sound of this island singing?
Is it the crackle of burning peat,
the hiss of sparks in bog power stations?
Is it the shatter of glass in recycling plants,
or squealing breaks, lovers' cries,
a dog's bark splitting the silence?

Is it the alley cat's warning, the bellow of deer,
the lullaby of rooks that blacken the horizon?
Is it the starlings tuning in spirits on long-wave,
or the banshee's wail,
drowned in white noise
and light pollution?

Is it the beep of cars locking, the click
of turning keys, the sigh of blinds
drawn down against the night,
the mosquito buzz of sodium lamps,
the whispered promises of radio presenters
that the news will be new tomorrow?

Is it the splash of boots through puddles,
the cutlery-clink of dishwashers,
the hum of prayers to God, or Allah,
or the pleas to saints or ancestors, *oh please*,
to intercede on our behalf?

Is it the song of a home far away,
hummed in tumbledown holiday camps?
Or the mutter of washing machines, TVs,

lit by the glow of tablets and phones
that fill the spaces between us?

Is it the warm song of an infant's breath?
Is it the cold music of stars rising
when the sun is extinguished
by sea?

II *The Parent's Song*

Each sleep is a miracle.
I lower the baby's fist
towards her chest
as it unclenches,
only for it to spring back
blackberry-firm,
for her arms to begin
the steam-paddle flail
that shoos away the night
and all its monsters.
How hard she works to keep
her eyes open, fixed on mine
in alarm as sleep settles
its ashes on her.
In her world a storm is raging –
her rest is a butterfly
flying ragged on the gale.
I take her hand,
wrap her fist in mine,
help her punch through
to a place petal-soft.

III *Song of the Wanderer*

My bed is a boat that floats
on dark water.

Once, you asked me to point
out the moon

and I found it below us,
troubled by waves.

I promised you
it was the same

as the one we watched
from the window back home.

I promised you
it would follow us

wherever we went –
never thinking

the moon
beneath the waves

would call you.
Never thinking

I would have
to dip my hand

beneath the surface
of sleep
        to hold yours.

IV *Song of the Insomniac*

Things I've counted
once sleep has fled,
scattering its sheep
through empty streets:

hatchling spiders
riding silk in the wind,
buds on a birch
in the cold March dawn,
a hedge-sparrow's feathers,
the barnacle geese –
their flight and return,
flight and return,
over empty playing fields.

When they've gone
I close my eyes and count
the snowflakes falling
in Sainte Foy,
on the Dolomites,
in Ruka and Oppdal.

And when sleep
comes to flirt
I walk on water,
count grains of plastic
in a plankton's gut
the whale's baleen,
the seas' glass bottles
with their messages of love,
all the songs in a sea-shell.

And back in our room
I tally the whorls
on your fingertips,
your eyelashes,
each flicker of the eyelid
that numbers
your dreams.

V *Song of the Night Worker*

The rain on the bus window
breaks the city into splinters.
Which one of them is hiding you?

I'm pulling the night with me,
let it slip from your shoulders,
see it snag the stars along its hem.

I'm tossing the dawn to you –
cup its flame in your palms
feed it your soft breath

fan it back to me across the miles,
so I can look up, where I am,
at the sky we share.

VI *Song of the Dawn*

It begins with a blackbird singing
in a cold laneway,
his yellow iris
the dawn's spark,

with dark slipping
away from the streets
revealing the shape of the day,
and the odes we sing

to each dull morning:
o crisp packet,
o empty can, o puddle
slick with oil, o morning

coughs and sighs, o cat
stretching a yoga pose.
O passing train, o soles
slapping a route to work,

o stale bread warmed to toast,
o orange juice, o coffee cup.
The island is stretching its limbs
beneath us, rolling us out

of our beds. O morning,
o each day's promise of return.
O song of lives
that are never still.

PIT LULLABY VI

Though in your infant state
you are soft, pink, malleable,
in rosebud mind

and curled-up body,
they will tell you all your life
that love is your best defense.

This is a lie that twists.

And when you are sad, they will offer you
the love of your friends
as if warmth is a privilege

denied those with power or wealth,
they will remind you you're safe
in the lap that cushions infants

till gender becomes cemented
and the boy children are dropped,
like chicks too worthless to sex,

into the blender,
forgotten by everyone
but tidy ranks of weeping mothers.

And so remember when you wield
your paper heart in a gale,
you're lucky to have
something beautiful
to lose
in the storm.

The Signs

beds in the great open-air sickbay
before and behind us

CAROLYN FORCHÉ

I *Graveyard*

On the outskirts of the city, we disappear –
just another woman and child
flitting down avenues to the graveyard.
We sit in the ruined church,
eat strawberries from a polythene bag.
A robin watches us from ivy, a blackbird
trills alarm. Bus drivers stroll and smoke.
The gravestone is our table,
and so we sit and eat with the dead,
their bones warm in the spring ground.

II *Banana Bread*

When civilisation breaks down,
the bananas are the first to go –
their skins bruising hickory
on sun-warmed windowsills –
so we mulch them into batter,
light the oven. Cinnamon warms
our kitchens. Small comforts
can be made from little deaths.

III *The Silence*

How did it begin?

The build to it was furious –
a world of kettles hissing,
saw-blades screeching through steel,
rooks coughing in the tree-tops.

It was a billion watts
of electricity humming
through an arterial web of wires,
it was infants' teeth grinding in the dark,

and the sound grew and grew
until every glass shattered,
and every dog howled,
and every car alarm wailed,
in one shuddering guffaw
belching out across the evening
before the silence sucked them in.

And like the sickness
of a broken bone
that recedes
to a white horizon of pain
the silence was worse
than what had come before.

IV *Binoculars*

My husband buys them for me,
we stare and stare into the garden.

> They bring the far walls closer, sprint
> the distance between cherry blossom,
> pine, and breeze-block.

They bring us fresh air,
crisp and flattened, hyper-real.

> We all have skinned knees and our hearts beat
> a hummingbird-buzz of anxiety –

skin bruises and mends, days pass.
The lens bends space and time around us,

> a ghost trips my daughter where she stands.

V *Night*

and someone is playing Beethoven
    while outside the dead wake,
        roll their bones from their graves
            through ditches and culverts,
                desperate to cross the water
                    and reunite in Europe's great ossuary.
                        Time reassemble us into what we once were,
        flesh creep back,
        eye-whites and lips.
      Oh faithful teeth I clench you to me
    to clatter in my rib cage while the stars
clash their cymbals.
There is harmony here,
    a calling forth, till the music stops
        and the dead settle exhausted
            into piles of white sticks
                among the nettles,
                    knowing they outnumber us.
                        A skull's jaw lolls in a collapsed grave,
                    still for now, till the the notes sound again
                across the blacked-out city.

VI *The Wood Between the Worlds*

When I came here today
I didn't realise you would follow,
but here you are, slipping through
pockets of syrup-light,
your skin pinking in the beams
that escape the leaves' net,
stopping somewhere out of sight
to cool your freckling shoulders in shadow.
Are you hiding from me, baby,
after trailing me so far?

I'll sit and wait for a flash of your hair,
all toffee and bronze, between the branches.
I'll sit by the pools and I'll watch for you.

If you can hear me, know
that one is *Mnemosyne* and one is *Lethe*.
One is there, and one is back-again.
And all are *left-alone*.
And all are *never-change*.

I would never have brought you
to this world of always evening, always leaving,
where you tell me you can hear
your brother and sister
call you from the far trees.

PIT LULLABY VII

When we turn off the light and I hold you close
your face becomes a puzzle – a wisp of hair
settling on a cheek, an eyebrow like a capstone

sinking in a restless sea. Here I whisper to you
broken thoughts that settle on the tangle
of our limbs. Mog sat in the dark and thought dark thoughts,

I say, because it is the only thing in any of your books
I recognise as true – a beast, alone out of doors,
and far from home. I lie in the dark

and think dark thoughts while your feet push my thighs away.
I make a weapon of the weight of my bones.
There are so many hours between us and the morning.

Nureyev in Dublin

As we drive, rain licks
the car's windows.
With each thunder crack
I'm shrieking
GOD IS ON THE TOILET,

and my mother's warnings
delivered with a static-sizzle,
raise hairs on my arms
to dancers on full point –

but something wonderful
is about to happen,
we are going to the ballet,
so my mother can unravel

her still-young frame,
folded like the coat hangers
my dad uses
to jimmy the car lock,

and she will dance
back through dislocated hips,
missed scholarships,
till she is pink-petalled confection.

But instead we get Nureyev,
ash-powdered, wire-thin,
weighted by sickness.
And I talk too loud,
bristle sweet papers;

take home on my shoulders
Nureyev's heavy legs,
and the stage, whispering
That's enough, now.
Enough flight.
Enough.

Holidaying with Dad During the Divorce

His car is a nervous breakdown,
scattering chrome along the motorway.
He gasps through panic attacks
in tunnels and medieval towers.
The falconry display goes on regardless
and eejits in velour have a crack
at each other with plywood lances.
I'm in fugue state, headphones glued
to me as mum calls to accuse him of kidnapping.
Come for a drink, he says.
No. Retreat to the Travelodge,
dry my one pair of decent flares
rancid from days of rain,
in the mysterious trouser press.
My anger flits and shifts
like a clot of starlings.
He presses into my hands
some Günter Grass,
and Sylvia Plath –
time-capsule messages
in a language we don't share,
and the evening heaves
with the bellow of cows
taken from their calves.

Dad Cars

Down into the mine we drive them,
leave them to rust into living rock.
The red Cortina bleached pink
headlights flicking on, off,
against quartz.

Then the Morris Minor,
a shadow at the pit's base –
we shake our heads, laugh
at how the floor fell out
on the motorway.

The aspirational Triumph,
its bonnet cop-car blue,
the chrome Dad loved
weeping rust into the water-table.

And the break-up Volvo
with its denial of sex,
like a divorcee dedicating
themselves to the worship
of their own boxy body,

the car that won't collapse,
that will sit in this cavern
sugar-coated with calcite,
till stalactites candle it
to a pipe organ.

I promise him: some day
I'll bury him here
in the oil-soaked sand,
a wing-mirror in each hand,

a battery block beneath his head,
and the last, unstolen car radio
singing

       in the mine's heart.

PIT LULLABY VIII

Something I need to tell you:
 it is true   *a tissue binds us*
like strings of yeast *rhizomes* *in a forest.*
Something we can't see *keeps us gathered*
     in these choked cities
  something so wide and deep
    we only see its shape
   when it's gone

Milk Teeth

Brutal organism
        you reduce me to blood
fret the boundaries
                between us to slip back in
                        through the nipple

but I won't let you in   no
        I'll wait   till those little workmen
with their files and wrenches
                settle around you   in the dark
to steal some
        of your ghastly enamel frill

here is something in return
        hard currency
                take it with you   line your pockets
        spill it on the earth
                like so many useless scales
and fingernails

but keep as my lasting gift
        two coins   for your eye teeth
take them to the river

Lessons

your birth   left me drenched in night sweats
grew the knowledge in me   that death was polishing coins for us
all those long pre-anaesthetic ages   ready to take us both
your shoulders shut   in the door-jamb of my pelvis
what strange skeletons   we would have made

and for a moment i was   the future ghost of all
those pale small girls   you picture in the background
in old novels where great men   are saying great things
i was a great pale tide   of little marys –

i tell a lie –   i first met death at 7   on the stairs of the 15 bus
he had no body but he lived   behind my eyes
swung space sideways   till i could see a thousand crashes
spiral out   and all the cold dead faces

and on the hourglass's wasp-cinched waist   there's you   as much
your father as you are me   and twice again yourself   double-helix spiralling
as the world turns and turns   phosphorous spark
in the great dark laboratory.

and after you?   i still see death on my left shoulder
ready to flip this egg timer world   but now
i save a space for you   inside me
i wear the skin   a little looser on my bones

Zodiac

And then there is the decade   when you will ask
for the first time   then over and over
who am i who am i who am i
and you will have been told   there is so much knowledge
in the world   sums and words and surgeries
soldering and nuclear power   the grand cathedral of it all
arching over you   hiding secrets in its darker corners
and somewhere in the distance   is the murmur
of some hierophant's words   you can't decipher
so you look to stars   to map your way
the froth of them dusted   across the vault
and raging/afraid you put   your fist through the glass
that separates you   from the sky's probing gaze
then curl up on a friend's bed   bleeding/confused
as to whether   *friend* and *fuck* are the same
so you hold hands   trace the goat the archer the virgin
like children directing   the glass on a Ouija board
then read to each other
the signs the signs the signs

Rock Pool

Baby, watch the hermit crabs
escape your bucket,
look at the everyday jewels
of their houses –
sand blown to glass.

See them flee from water,
drown in air
like your gasping cries on days
when we fail to meet
your implacable need –

my periwinkle. My limpet.
Our crab-tango.
Now watch your grandfather,
on days when names
side-step him in shallows,

tangle in the seaweed of his hair,
drip in the salt-water trail
he traipses through the house.
On bad days, salt-crust
on our cheeks.

The world finds its golden mean;
here are its pincers
                        bearing down,
pinning each beginning to its end.

Turbulence

The cup judders in my hand
and the Russians beside me
fall silent.

In this slender cigar, we crouch
as if our stillness
might calm the air outside,

and I am Caliban, spirit-stoked.
my words a curse or a howl;
what could I summon

from my well of understanding
to put meaning on a death
so far away from you?

What does the mother
three rows back whisper
into her sleeping baby's ear?

Can someone, in the moments
it will take for us
to topple from the sky,

for us to splash star-like on the ground,
for lit gasoline to obliterate
our eyes and teeth,

in those precious seconds,
can someone teach me
that language?

PIT LULLABY IX

And	who	else	is here	in	the	dark?
who	else	is here	in	the	dark?	
else	is here	in	the	dark?		
is here	in	the	dark?			
in	the	dark?				
the	dark?					
dark?						

JUDITH KERR, *Mog in the Dark*

Apples are here in the dark
waiting for teeth to shred flesh,
eat them to the core,
ink-black pips turned over
in small tight fists as hours drag by –
tiny eyes shut tight,
dark planets in orbit.

Worms are here in the dark,
eating and excreting the dirt
I grind from the treads of your shoes.
I'm terrified by your body's invitation to harm,
terrified of dog shit and blindness –
darkness that could creep out of the pit
and into your pockets.

Elephants are here in the dark,
infinite rows of them, tuskless and starving,
indris clinging to burning trees,
turtles scrabbling on midnight beaches,
dashed under the tyres of cars,
albatrosses' guts and beaks trussed in plastic,
weathered into shapes no one sees.

Ink is here in the dark,
indigo plants and woad stems pulverised,
trickling into the air until it blackens,
drawing all remaining light into a pinprick,
a halo I can hold behind closed eyelids.
Wait for it to fade as the dye workers
end their shift; the skies now pitch.

In the dark? Me? Yes I must be here,
tracing and retracing my steps,
dancing sometimes to prove I'm not dead
and even the dead must dance
when the mood takes them,
even bones can ring a true note
in the right hands.

Trees are here in the dark,
deaf and blind to the absence of light,
and leaves are here in spite of the dark,
wood and wind and music, somehow,
every time the breeze blows
in the sunless meadows,
in the nothing much.

Dark is here in the dark,
and it is an absence, so how do
we hold it? Shape it like clay?
Every darkness has its enclosure,
its doors and windows to shut –
it keeps the light out.
Try to be the shape that holds the dark.

Hungry Ghost

I

My husband the sugar merchant
is stingy with his sweetness,

locks his loaves in a storeroom
since the night he caught me naked,

running the edge of my tongue
the length of one long cone,

my spittle glinting a path
to the summit, and whipped me

with a bamboo switch until I bled.
When the wandering monk arrives,

dribbling into his robe,
my husband unhooks his key,

hands it to me. I look him
in the eye, measure the memory

of my thighs, sticky
with resin and blood.

II

The monk settles
into his own stink,

witters prayers, waiting
for his cup of sugar-water.

I unlock the store room,
slice a snowfall into his bowl.

The light in the room, so white,
so pure, makes a joke of the monk –

his filthy robes, his liar's eyes –
so I piss in his portion,

watch the stream splash
the sides of the sugar-cone gold.

The dirty fucker gulps it down
and I laugh and laugh –

till my throat cramps,
my voice vanishes,

my eyes crust
with glucose.

III

My husband beats me
many more nights after that,

but what tortures me is the hunger
that hollows me, makes music

on my rib cage, bird's wings
from the span of my hands,

when all I can find to eat are
pints of frosting, gallons of syrup.

The monk's prayers rattle around me
like bats at dusk,

and my walls run with nectar –
anything for a bitter morsel.

Bilbea's Response

You ask why I don't write?
The towers all on fire
and the plague-fleas dancing
on the rats and you ask
why I don't think of you?

Maybe I wrote your name
with menstrual blood
on the Ishtar gate.
Maybe a half-starved bastard
in an alley bears your name.

Maybe though I simply forgot
one cock among many
and even a kind word or two
wasn't enough to allow you entry
to the small store of memories I keep.

Lock Years

In my teenage years I started forging locks
from anything I found lying around
I thought chakras were bullshit –
but a useful map –
so I began.

For my base, base metal –
a chain of paperclips twisted,
a chastity belt
pricking beads of blood
from thigh and labia.

For my navel, a thousand
chocolate wrappers, bars sucked thin,
a tattered flag of primary colours,
jumbled text with no message
but ache and hunger.

For my chest, an underwire
to pinch my armpits,
to girdle my breasts
and cover the light
in my ribcage.

For my throat, a song
I sang whenever questions were asked,
a lie and then another lie felted
into a scarf I stuffed
into my mouth.

For my brow, a nest of tweezers,
and mascara brushes, layers and layers
of eyeliner to distract
from the hole in my forehead
where the thoughts leaked out.

And for my crown,
a web of roots,
maggot white,
reaching down
to bind my feet.

Onion Poem

Lately I can't stop thinking of the nun's
yearly speech in school assembly
about peeling another layer of the onion
and how I feel I'm trapped
between the onion's bitter layers –
this layer, the ball of uncried tears
my mother says is the cause of my asthma,
this layer, the skin of youth,
lifting and cracking to scuttle
across my kitchen floor,
this one, the taste I wake with
after another night of constant feeding,
my baby satisfied, but I am I am I am
always thirsty,
then this spindle at the centre
one end rooting, one end browning into rot.
It always struck me as a brutal metaphor –
to tear away the onion's peach-fuzz membrane –
flensing was the word that sang
in my mind, which when I looked it up
turned out to mean *slicing the skin or meat
from a carcass*, and yes, that is what happened to us,
the whole school body,
we were flensed into adulthood –
pearl-skins falling from us,
and no one allowed to cry.

In the Bathroom Showroom

No one seems to be able to see us,
the art of invisibility impressive
given our toddler's shouted refrain
of MAMA HALP MAMA HAT
while waving her neon baseball cap.

Among the charcoal vanity units
and baths seeping albumen light,
we are so very specific, a many-edged
chaos algorithm that spills and wobbles
and occasionally screeches,
CAH-CO-DILE!

But when we judder back out
through the green tinted glass,
on our comedy wheels,
nothing at all achieved, there's
the struggle of a tiny bird
trapped in a corner –

and between us, we crouch like hunters
throw a hoodie ('Shh! We have a plan')
take our bundle out into the car park's
concrete layer-cake where –
Look! We gift to the day

a small explosion of pied wagtail,
conjured from dada's jacket.
Fair play! says the car park attendant –
at my daughter's bemused pleasure.
What treasures might she expect now?

Hunting Lions

Beasts stalk these streets –
they must, or why would we take such care
to avoid our neighbours?

Now, I don't have to tell you to move aside
when people pass us on the pavement.
It's hardwired, and you're forgetting the names

of the playschool friends you missed those first weeks.
But you know there's something off-kilter,
and so each day we sneak into the park,

ready to hunt. Sometimes you startle
at sounds I can't hear, and the hairs on my arms
rise like thistledown on a breeze.

One day I'll turn and see him there,
the lion you have been hunting,
feel his breath sweat-heavy on my neck.

Hawthorn

We clamber up a grass-pocked mound of earth –
Watch, there's nettles. Be careful. Hold my hand –
but you slip away, scouring the park
for something, haring up and down
this pint-size mountain,
raising cabbage whites from ragwort,
shaking dandelion clocks. The trees
hold your gaze, the closest one a hawthorn,
smothered in whipped drifts of flowers.
My brother is in the tree, you say,
and you're gone again before I can ask
how the idea of a brother could take root in you.
Some old cunning turns in me,
and I pull a clump of low hanging flowers,
breathe their tang of sex and death –
leave them on our doorstep to wither overnight,
a May charm against changelings, or harm.

Night Run

Come to my bed in the pewter hours
between sleeping and waking, like a doctor
on the night round. Place your hand
over my eyes and let me see. There,
my own feet. How they've moved me.
Raise my chin so I can see a path ahead,
through willowherb and bloody cranesbill,
the river stitching itself into air,
midges tracing equations on the breeze.
Hold my hand while I run, as if we're
the only moving things on this spinning world,
chasing the dusk so the evening stays golden.
Lace me back into my arms and guide them,
breathe the earth's heat into my toes. I'll race you
for as long as you'll follow.

PIT LULLABY X

She knows it must be there,
Knows the shape that corrals the bright
Yellowing clouds that pass over
Like the ghosts who whisper
In our ears while we dream,
Gliding from our eye-line when we wake.
Here is mother, asleep. And here's the sky,
Touching us, even when our eyes are closed.

Lullaby

I have a lullaby for you at last,
so lie beside me, hold my hand,
follow me through the night's amber lens
to Bull Island.
Here, the seals are waking
from their sleep, rolling into the surf
where in blue-black
they'll stretch the land-ache
from their muscles.
Here, the only touch is water.
Moonlight on scale. Dazzle of bubbles.
Blubber's cape and fish blood's
meagre warmth. These are my notes,
the strand our stave.
Our music rises and falls,
we are waveform; we are sea.

NOTES

Forecast (39): Lines in italics are taken from the *Annals of the Four Masters*, chronicles of medieval Irish history.

Hungry Ghost (77): Jikininki (食人鬼 'human-eating ghosts') in Japanese mythology are the spirits of people who were greedy or selfish in life, and are cursed to eat human corpses after death.

Bilbea's Response (80): A response to 'Bilbea' by Carl Sandburg.

ACKNOWLEDGEMENTS

Thanks are due to the following journals and their editors who featured versions of these poems: *Banshee, Butcher's Dog, Empty House* (Friends of the Earth), *The London Magazine, Magma, The Music of What Happens* (New Island), *The North, One* (Jacar Press), *Poetry Ireland Review, The Stinging Fly, TriQuarterly, Verseville, The Winter Papers V* and *Women on Nature* (Unbound). 'On Plastics' was highly commended in the 2020 Ginkgo Prize.

Poems from the collection were also featured on the *Words Lightly Spoken* podcast, *The Poetry Jukebox, The Poetry Programme* (RTÉ) and *Sunday Miscellany* (RTÉ). 'A Plea for the Sanctification of the Ditches of Ireland' was commissioned by Rockfinch Productions and BBC Radio 4 for *My Modest Proposal*, broadcast in March 2020.

'Hunting Lions' and 'Hawthorn' were commissioned by Dún Laoghaire-Rathdown County Council for the Artworks Home series. 'On Poisons' and 'The Signs' were commissioned by The Salvage Press for publication in limited edition letterpress art books. 'Forecast' was commissioned by The Yeats Society, Sligo, to celebrate the centenary of the publication of 'The Second Coming' by W.B. Yeats. 'Milk Teeth' was commissioned by The Model, Sligo, in response to their 2021 exhibition *The Body Electric*. 'An Island Sings' was commissioned by Poetry Ireland and Chamber Choirs Ireland, and was set to music by composer Elaine Agnew and performed by choirs from the four provinces of Ireland in March 2019 at the National Concert Hall in Dublin.

Thanks to Culture Ireland and the Ireland Literature Exchange for financial support for trips overseas, and to Carlow College, Carlow County Council and VISUAL Carlow, Dún Laoghaire-Rathdown County Council, and The Yeats Society, Sligo, for commissions and residencies in recent years.

Special thanks to Elaine Feeney, Conor O'Callaghan and Dean Browne for the craic and the chats about poems, and as always to Jane Clarke, Eithne Hand, Catherine Phil McCarthy and Rosamund Taylor for being my first and best readers. And finally, to Declan, Abigail and Isobel, all my love.